# 21ST CENTURY DEBATES

# CLIMATE CHANGE
## OUR IMPACT ON THE PLANET

## SIMON SCOONES

HODDER
Wayland

an imprint of Hodder Children's Books

## 21st Century Debates Series

| | | | |
|---|---|---|---|
| Air Pollution | Endangered Species | Energy | Climate Change |
| Food Supply | Genetics | Internet | Media |
| Population Explosion | Rainforests | Surveillance | Waste, Recycling and Reuse |

Produced for Hodder Wayland by White-Thomson Publishing Ltd, 2/3 St Andrew's Place, Lewes, East Sussex, BN7 1UP

© 2001 White-Thomson Publishing Ltd

Published in Great Britain in 2001 by Hodder Wayland, an imprint of Hodder Children's Books.

Editor: Philippa Smith
Commissioning editor: Polly Goodman
Proofreader: Hazel Songhurst
Series design: Mind's Eye Design, Lewes
Artwork: Peter Bull Art Studio, William Donohoe and Tim Mayer

A catalogue record for this book is available from the British Library.

ISBN 0 7502 3269 2

Printed and bound in Italy by G. Canale & C.S.p.A., Turin.

Hodder Children's Books, a division of Hodder Headline Ltd, 338 Euston Road, London NW1 3BH

Picture acknowledgements: Associated Press 23 (Subir Haldar), 58 (Serge Ligtenberg), cover foreground (Kent Gilbert); CORBIS 9 (David Muench), 18, 21 (Reuters/NewMedia Inc), 28 (Galen Rowell), 29 (Reuters/ NewMedia Inc), 34 and 35 (Michael & Patricia Fogden), 38 (Dan Gurevich), 44 (Kelly-Mooney Photography), 54 (Gary Braasch), 55 (Kevin R Morris); Ecoscene 37 (John Liddiard), 59 (Chinch Gryniewicz); Chris Halls 41; Robert Harding Picture Library 17 (Victor Engelbert); HWPL 13 (inset/ Chris Fairclough), 46 (Tony Morrison), 57 (Richard Sharpley); Panos Pictures 25 (Piers Benatar); Ed Parker 27; Photodisc Inc 11, cover background; Popperfoto 22 (Yuri Cortez), 24 (Silvia Izquierdo), 48 (Mufty Munir), 52 (Reuters/Dylan Martinez); Science Photo Library 7 (NASA/Goddard Space Flight Control), 16 (NOAA); Simon Scoones 32; Still Pictures 12 (Ingrid Moorjohn), 13 (main photo/Nigel Dickinson), 14 (Joerg Boethling), 15 (John Isaac), 20 (Mark Edwards), 30-31 (Jeff Greenberg), 33 (Shehzad Nooran), 36 (Fred Bavendam), 40 (S Cytrynowicz-Christian Aid), 42 (Hartmut Schwarzbach), 43 and 45 (Mark Edwards), 47 (Tantyo Bangun), 49 (Albert Visage), 50 (Mark Edwards), 53 (Paul Gipe), 56 (Jeff Greenberg). Illustrations on page 10 by Peter Bull Art Studio, on pages 4, 5, 15 and 33 by William Donohoe, and on pages 6 and 19 by Tim Mayer.

Cover: Foreground picture shows a Costa Rican man fighting the currents from flood waters as he flees his house. In 1996, the heavy rains that accompanied Hurricane Cesar caused extensive floods and landslides throughout Costa Rica. Background picture shows cloud cover over the Earth recorded by satellite. Satellite technology enables a more detailed and accurate picture of climate change.

# CONTENTS

What is Climate Change? .............................................4

Causes of Climate Change: Natural or Human? ........10

El Niño and La Niña .................................................16

A Weather of Extremes?.............................................20

Rising Sea Levels .....................................................28

Warning Signs from the Natural World....................34

Feeding the World ...................................................40

Climate Change and Human Health.......................46

International Co-operation .......................................52

Glossary...................................................................60

Books and CD-Roms ...............................................61

Addresses.................................................................62

Index .......................................................................63

# WHAT IS CLIMATE CHANGE?

## Weather or climate?

We have all experienced days when rain has spoiled a barbecue or a heatwave draws us to the beach. We have also read about dramatic floods and hurricanes that disrupt people's lives. These events could be just unusual changes in the weather, the day-to-day pattern of our atmosphere. Farmers, airline pilots, ships' captains and organizers of outside sports events all rely on information about the weather to plan their daily operations. By collecting information on the daily weather conditions an average, long-term pattern of the temperature, precipitation, humidity, wind and cloudiness of a place can be worked out. This is called its climate.

### The power of the Sun

The most important influence on the climate of any area is its position relative to the Sun. The Sun beams down rays that bring energy to Earth in the form of heat. Around the Equator, the Sun is overhead and here the Earth is nearest the Sun. As a result, equatorial areas receive more solar energy, so equatorial climates have hot temperatures all year. Once heated the air rises, and winds and ocean currents carry the warmth to higher and lower latitudes, sharing out some of this solar energy. Further north and south of the Equator the Sun's energy is spread over a wider area and the distance from the Sun is greater. These regions receive less solar energy and so have a cooler climate.

*The energy of the Sun's rays is more concentrated at the Equator and the Tropics than at the Poles, where it is spread over a wider area.*

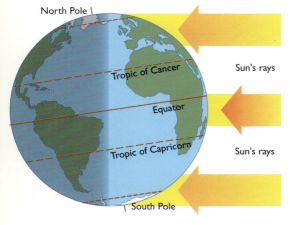

North Pole

Tropic of Cancer

Sun's rays

Equator

Tropic of Capricorn

Sun's rays

South Pole

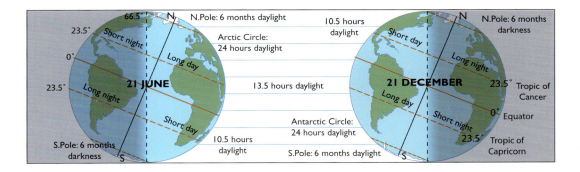

## Changes in the seasons

The tilt of the Earth relative to the Sun, and its orbit around the Sun during the year, means that climate is seasonal. In June, the northern hemisphere is tilted towards the Sun and receives more hours of sunshine and warmth than the southern hemisphere, which is tilted away. At this time it is summer in the northern hemisphere and winter in the southern hemisphere. By December, the Earth has orbited half way round the Sun so that the southern hemisphere is now tilted towards the Sun and enjoys summer, while the northern hemisphere is tilted away from the Sun, and has colder, winter weather. People who live in very northern latitudes can experience up to 24 hours of darkness at this time of year.

## The influence of the mountains and the oceans

The climate of a place is also influenced by other factors, such as altitude and its nearness to the sea. Above very high land, the atmosphere contains less dust and water vapour, so heat rises and escapes more quickly than at lower altitudes. Coastal areas are affected by the temperature of the sea. As water takes longer to heat up or cool down than land, coastal areas can be warmed by the warmer sea air during the winter, and cooled by the cooler sea air during the summer. This means that people who live along coasts have a less extreme climate.

*The Earth's tilted orbit around the Sun means that when it is winter in the northern hemisphere it is summer in the southern hemisphere, and vice versa.*

## VIEWPOINT

'The climate where I live has a great influence on my life. During the summer it is warm and sunny enough to grow corn and vegetables, and I let my dairy cows roam the pastures. But during the winter we have to keep our cows indoors because it is too cold and dark for them outside.'
*Thrine Sofie Omli. farmer in Nord Arnoy Island. northern Norway*

## Key

- 🔴 Tropical climate (hot and wet)
- 🟡 Dry climate (hot and dry)
- 🟢 Mild climate (warm and wet)
- 🟣 Continental climate (cold and wet)
- ⚪ Polar climate (very cold and dry)
- 🟤 Mountainous areas where altitude makes it cooler and brings more rain and snow

*This map shows how the world can be divided into six climate zones.*

In the oceans, ocean currents, the huge volumes of water that are constantly moving, can influence the climate too. The current known as the Gulf Stream, for example, carries warm water away from the tropical Caribbean northwards and warms the east coast of the USA. It then crosses the Atlantic to Europe. This warm water in turn heats up winds that blow across it, taking the chill out of winters in western Europe. These different influences on the Earth's surface lead to a range of climate zones.

## Measuring the weather

Meteorologists have been using instruments like thermometers, rain gauges, anemometers and barometers to record changes in temperature, rainfall, wind speed and air pressure at weather stations for over 300 years, and still do so today. However, since 1960, scientists have also benefited from the use of satellites in space to understand how the Earth's atmosphere works. Satellites can provide a global picture of conditions on the Earth's surface so, for the first time, scientists could gather information on the weather in remote areas, such as the middle of oceans and the polar ice caps. This allows meteorologists to forecast weather patterns more accurately.

Geostationary satellites orbit at 36,000 km above the Equator. As they complete one orbit every 24 hours they continually look down on the same part of the Earth. Polar-orbiting satellites, on the other hand, are positioned closer to the Earth's surface and view the atmosphere from different angles throughout the day. Satellite images of the Earth can be downloaded to weather stations every half an hour. This sophisticated technology makes it possible to track the path of a hurricane across an ocean, or to see drought conditions developing in the Horn of Africa.

## Measuring climate change

Nowadays, scientists are also able to use sophisticated technology to reveal changes in past climate. By drilling deep down into the ice sheets of Antarctica, scientists can extract columns of ice, called ice cores, that have built up over thousands of years as snow has been compressed. They can study the water molecules and composition of gases trapped in the layers of ice to discover what the climate was like in Antarctica hundreds of thousands of years ago. It is also possible to study tree growth rings to find out about past climate changes. Trees produce a growth ring each year; the distance between the rings depends largely on how warm the climate was at the time. To discover what climates were like even further back, the fossilized remains of animals and plants that lived in a particular area can be studied to reveal what their environment was like millions of years ago.

*A 3D computer image, based on data from the American GOES-9 satellite, of Hurricane Linda off the coast of Mexico in 1997. The hole in the centre is the 'eye' of the storm, an area of calm air and very low pressure. Around the eye, winds reached 300 kph.*

## Climate change is nothing new

With all this information from past and present, scientists can piece together a picture of climate change. We now know that the climate of the Earth has changed constantly throughout the history of the planet over millions of years. No matter where you live, the climate is always changing to some degree, but some changes are less predictable than others. A small wobble in the Earth's orbit around the Sun can lead to small changes in global temperatures, but this can cause more floods, hurricanes or heatwaves than normal. A volcanic eruption can also temporarily alter the world's climate; after the eruption of Mount Pinatubo, in 1991, the amount of dust particles that entered the atmosphere blocked out some of the Sun's heat, cooling the world's temperature for a year or so.

## Predicting the future

Meteorologists can now use computers to analyze the information from satellites and develop models to predict the climate in the future. However, this is not an exact science. Some meteorologists do not trust these computer models because they are based on mathematical formulae rather than actual data. It is also possible for meteorologists to interpret the results of a computer model to predict different outcomes.

## Is there any need to worry?

The burning question is whether the changes in our climate today are part of a much bigger and more dramatic shift in climate that will affect the way we live on Earth. More and more scientists have been concerned over small changes in global temperatures that were recorded during the twentieth century, the effects this may have on life on Earth and what is causing these changes. Newspapers have been predicting disasters that may lie ahead as a result. In 1988, alarm amongst

*In 1988, unusual snowfalls in Monument Valley, USA, surprised US meteorologists, sparking more debate over whether the climate is changing faster than was previously thought.*

world leaders over climate change led them to set up the Intergovernmental Panel on Climate Change (IPCC), pulling together 2,000 scientists from all over the world. One of the scientists' jobs was to look at available information on climate change. For example, are recent climate changes the result of another natural cycle, or are the actions of human beings responsible? The truth is that not all scientists agree.

## DEBATE

As there remains a lot of uncertainty over whether or not climate changes in recent years are something to worry about, should we just relax for now and wait until scientists have more definite proof?

# CAUSES OF CLIMATE CHANGE: NATURAL OR HUMAN?

## Greenhouse Earth

Scientists have found out that when there are changes in global temperatures, changes in the concentrations of certain gases in the atmosphere occur as well. This suggests that there is a link between the two. When the Sun's energy reaches the Earth, a layer of gases that surrounds the planet filters the Sun's rays and prevents big swings in temperature.

*The 'greenhouse effect': as greenhouse gases in the atmosphere increase, less heat escapes back into space and more is trapped near the Earth's surface, causing global warming.*

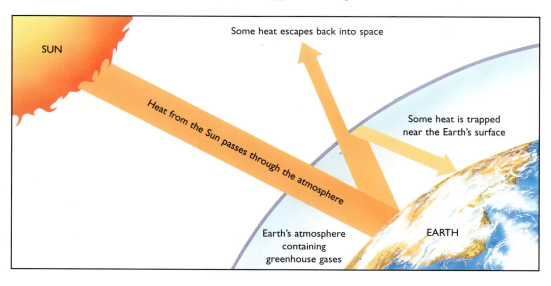

SUN

Some heat escapes back into space

Heat from the Sun passes through the atmosphere

Some heat is trapped near the Earth's surface

Earth's atmosphere containing greenhouse gases

EARTH

These gases stop too much heat from getting in and too much heat from escaping, rather like the effect of glass in a greenhouse. However, we can have too much of a good thing, as an excess of these gases could disrupt the climate patterns on Earth. The IPCC scientists believe that an increase of these greenhouse gases will trap too much heat nearer the Earth's surface and lead to a rise in global temperatures. This is known as 'global warming'.

## Natural gases

The main greenhouse gas that occurs naturally is the water vapour evaporated from rivers, lakes, seas and oceans, and the moisture lost from plant and animal species. Water vapour acts like a blanket in the lower atmosphere, trapping the Sun's heat beneath it. The heat that escapes through the water vapour can be trapped by gases that form another layer higher up in the atmosphere. Carbon dioxide ($CO_2$), which is in the air we breathe, is the most important of these gases.

## VIEWPOINT

'Greenhouse gases naturally present in the atmosphere act like an insulating blanket over the Earth and help warm the planet. Without them the average temperature on Earth would be a chilly minus 18°C.'

*Dr Sallie Baliunas, Chair of the Science Advisory Board, George C Marshall Institute, USA*

*Some natural events, such as volcanic eruptions, add vast quantities of carbon dioxide ($CO_2$) to the atmosphere.*

## FACT

During the eruptions of Mount Etna in Sicily between 1975 and 1987, the volcano released about 25 million tonnes of carbon dioxide ($CO_2$) a year, the equivalent of four large coal-fired power stations.

As well as carbon dioxide, other gases from natural sources contribute to the greenhouse effect. For example, rotting plant material in marshes and swamps releases methane, while tropical forests give off nitrogen oxide. Both gases enter the atmosphere.

## Are people upsetting the balance?

Many scientists are now worried that the actions of people are increasing the amount of greenhouse gases, and could be changing the climate. People contribute to the layer of gases in the atmosphere by using fossil fuels like oil, coal and natural gas. When these fossil fuels are burned they release large quantities of $CO_2$, much of which escapes and hangs around in the atmosphere for up to 200 years. Industrialized countries, such as the USA, UK and Russia, have been using fossil fuels to provide power for factories and homes since the Industrial Revolution, and collectively they are believed to be responsible for most of the $CO_2$ emissions in the past. Now, many developing countries are choosing a similar path of development, using these resources to fuel the growth of their own industries and to satisfy the growing needs of their people.

*Over some cities in China the air is thick with the polluting gases pumped out from power stations and industries. These gases include $CO_2$.*

*Natural rainforests in tropical areas (inset) play an important role in absorbing $CO_2$, yet across the world people are destroying them at an alarming rate.*

## Trees as sinks

Trees naturally absorb $CO_2$ as part of their life cycle, acting like a 'sink' to soak up the gas. This has always helped to control the amount of $CO_2$ in the atmosphere. But economic development has disrupted the role that trees play in this way. Across the planet, people are destroying forests to provide land for new settlements and farmland, to extract resources like oil and gold, and to harvest the trees for valuable timber. This has meant that 80 per cent of the world's original forests have been cut down or badly damaged, and nearly half of the remaining forests are under threat. What is worse is that setting fire to the trees is one of the main methods of clearance. Half of every tree is made up of carbon and this is only released when the tree is burned. As a result, some scientists believe that burning forests may release as much $CO_2$ into the atmosphere as burning fossil fuels.

*Rice planting in India. During the production of rice, the old stalks of rice plants and other plant material rot in the paddy field water because they are deprived of fresh air. As they rot they release methane gas.*

## FACT

**'People carriers' and four-wheel-drives represent half the market of new cars in the USA. This new style of vehicle burns twice as much fuel as smaller cars, releasing more nitrogen oxides into the atmosphere.**

## Adding to the greenhouse effect

What is certain is that people are responsible for releasing other greenhouse gases, some of which cannot be avoided. In the East, rice-growing gives off large quantities of methane as organic matter decays in the rice paddies. Meanwhile, nearly 100 million tonnes of methane a year is generated by cattle as they digest their food.

Nitrogen oxides are a group of greenhouse gases that are another by-product of economic development. As more and more vehicles are used to transport people and goods from place to place, nitrogen oxides are released from the combustion of fossil fuels in the engines. These gases are also discharged in industrial processes and by nitrate fertilizers used on the land to boost crop harvests.

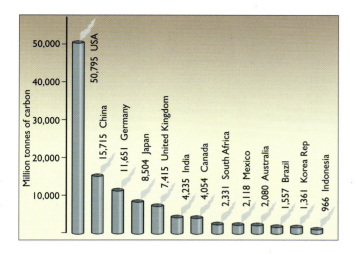

*Total carbon emissions of different countries 1950–1996. The diagram shows that the biggest polluters are mostly found in the developed world. However, there is a growing number of newly industrialized countries that are becoming major polluters as well.*

Since the 1950s, a group of man-made gases known as CFCs has been added to the list of greenhouse gases. CFCs are produced from coolants used in refrigerators and air conditioners, and they used to be released from aerosol cans and certain types of

*During the last days of the 1991 Gulf War, retreating Iraqi troops set alight most of the oil wells in Kuwait. About 240 million tonnes of $CO_2$ were released as the oil burned.*

foam packaging. Although the quantities of CFCs entering the atmosphere have been considerably less than other greenhouse gases, they stay in the atmosphere for several thousand years and could therefore cause global warming over a longer period of time. CFCs also contribute to another serious problem by destroying the layer of ozone that protects our planet from harmful Sun's rays.

## DEBATE

Do you think we should all change the way we live to reduce the amount of gases we add to the 'greenhouse'? If so, what changes should we make?

# EL NIÑO AND LA NIÑA

## El Niño

Changes in the layer of gases in the atmosphere, whether they be a result of natural or human causes, happen very slowly. However, thanks to the latest satellite technology, scientists are learning more about short-term changes in the world's climate caused by the interaction between the surface layers of the oceans and the atmosphere immediately above them. These changes have been particularly noticeable in the Pacific, the world's biggest ocean.

### The pull of the Pacific

In most years, strong, steady winds called trade winds blow westwards across the tropical Pacific Ocean towards Asia and Australasia. These winds drag and pile up the warm surface water in the west Pacific, making the sea surface warmer and about 0.5 m

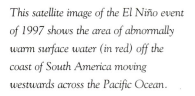

*This satellite image of the El Niño event of 1997 shows the area of abnormally warm surface water (in red) off the coast of South America moving westwards across the Pacific Ocean.*

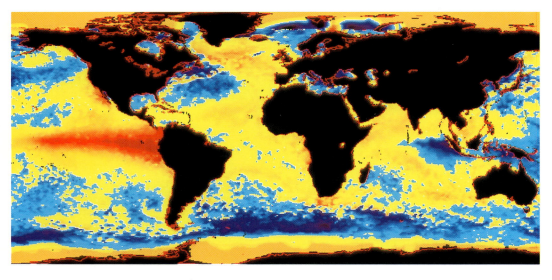

higher around the equatorial coasts of Indonesia and Australia compared to the equatorial coast of South America in the east. This huge patch of warm water (the size of the USA) evaporates, creating moist air that rises, cools and then condenses to bring rain to Indonesia and Australia. Meanwhile, on the eastern side of the ocean, there is an upwelling of colder water from the ocean depths to replace the surface water that has been dragged away. This cold surface water chills the air above it and the cold, dense air cannot rise high enough for the water vapour to condense into rain, with the result that the South American coast stays fairly dry.

Catches of fish such as anchovies are essential to the coastal communities of northern Peru, both as a source of food and as a way of making money.

## A warm Christmas

Hundreds of years ago, fishermen in boats off the coast of Peru noticed that every few years around December their fishing waters were unusually warm. This climate change was named El Niño, meaning 'the little boy' or 'Christ child' in Spanish because it seemed to start here around Christmas. The reasons for El Niño are not easy to understand but scientists have discovered that, every two to seven years, the interaction between the ocean waters and the atmosphere above becomes unstable, and this weakens the power of the trade winds. As a result, the trade winds do not have the strength to pull the warmer water westwards across the Pacific, so it remains nearer South America. This means that the temperatures and rainfall patterns of the ocean waters on either side of the Pacific are altered. A warm belt of water spreads right across the equatorial Pacific with warmer, wetter weather on the western side and cooler, drier weather on the eastern side.

### VIEWPOINT

'Buoys in the Pacific are now fixed up with the most sophisticated weather equipment way out in the ocean. We can now get a much more accurate picture of how El Niño behaves.'
*Bob Wade, meteorologist, San Diego, California, USA*

### FACT

According to the UK Meteorological Office, 1999 was a much cooler year than 1998 (the hottest year on record) because of La Niña.

## La Niña: a reversal of fortune

After an El Niño period, the trade winds can become stronger again, and sometimes they can drag even more warm surface water to the west, leaving behind a huge 'cold tongue' of ocean in the east. This cold tongue can spread further north, bringing drier, colder weather to North America as far up as Canada and Alaska. Meanwhile Australia's extra warm water brings them heavier rainfall. This reverse of El Niño is known as La Niña, 'little girl', and occurs about half as often as El Niño. The two together are seen as a cycle of climate change as the body of warm water moves back and forth, or 'oscillates' across the Pacific. This is known as the 'El Niño Southern Oscillation' (ENSO), where El Niño is the warm phase and La Niña is the cold phase of the ENSO.

## Investigating El Niño and La Niña

At the moment, no one is quite sure what causes an El Niño to start, and what makes some El Niño years stronger than others. To try to discover the onset of El Niño or La Niña, scientists have to keep a check on changes in the sea temperatures across the Pacific. Buoys are stationed across the vast ocean to collect accurate measurements of weather conditions. These are beamed back by satellite to meteorological stations on land.

*In 1998–99, La Niña could have been responsible for the more severe winter weather experienced in parts of North America.*

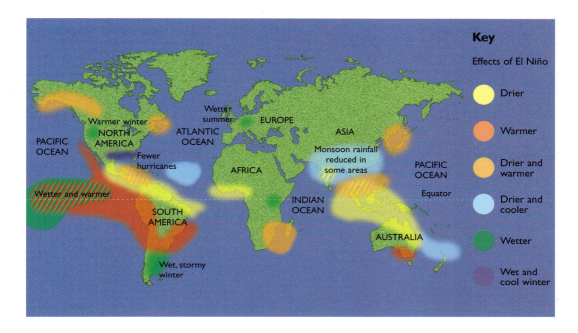

This map shows the areas of the world that experienced changes in their usual climate during 1998. Many scientists believe these changes were the result of El Niño.

Scientists also receive information from research ships criss-crossing the ocean. To see how frequent and how strong the ENSO was in the past, scientists can look back through ships' log books and read the diaries of fishermen in the Pacific.

## The spread of El Niño and La Niña

Scientists now know that the effects of El Niño and La Niña are not just felt in the Pacific – the changes in the strength of these easterly trade winds has a ripple effect on the climate patterns across the world. Changes in the wind and rainfall in the Pacific affect the atmosphere in the Indian Ocean further west, so that there are similar signs of El Niño and La Niña. This in turn has a knock-on effect on weather conditions in the Atlantic, west of the Indian Ocean. However, these oceans are smaller, and the larger land masses have more influence on the climate, so the effects of the ENSO are usually weaker. El Niño and La Niña are the most powerful phenomena on Earth, and alter the climate across more than half the planet.

## DEBATE

As the effects of El Niño seem to be getting stronger, do you think more money should be spent on warning people at risk of the onset of El Niño?

# A WEATHER OF EXTREMES?

*If environments where conditions are already hot and dry become even hotter, only the hardiest of plants, like this baobab tree, may survive.*

## New records are set

Changes in the layer of gases in the atmosphere and in the circulation of air above the Pacific in El Niño and La Niña periods have encouraged scientists to make many predictions about what will happen to weather patterns. In recent years, new records have been set in extreme weather events, and scientists believe that this is just the beginning. We may experience many more unpredictable, intense weather events in the future as the climate becomes more unstable.

### Getting hotter . . .

According to the Intergovernmental Panel on Climate Change (IPCC), nine of the hottest years since records began have occurred since 1988, with faster temperature rises than at any other time in the last 10,000 years, particularly at the Poles. Global warming is thought to be affecting the Arctic far more than other regions of the world, with temperatures rising three to five times faster. The ice cap is melting so quickly that climatologists have predicted that within 50 years it will disappear totally during the summer.

Based on current estimates of greenhouse gases in the atmosphere the IPCC also predicted that temperatures would continue to rise between 1.5 °C and 4.5 °C during the twenty-first century. To make things worse, rises in temperature may cause more evaporation and therefore more water vapour in the

global atmosphere. As water vapour is itself a greenhouse gas, the Earth could get even hotter.

## Getting drier . . .

For people that live in colder climates, the thought of longer, hotter summers may seem like an appealing future, but the impact will not be the same across the planet. For many other parts of the world, higher temperatures could be very serious. Interior areas, like the Great Plains of North America and parts of Africa, may endure longer and more frequent droughts. Already, western Africa has experienced temperatures much higher than it would normally expect, and drought is becoming a real problem. In areas where trees have been cut down, the lack of water vapour released from the trees' leaves could lead to less rainfall, higher temperatures and possible drought.

### VIEWPOINTS

'You can't draw any conclusions about long-term global climate trends based on a heatwave here and a cold snap there.'
*John Christy, Professor of Atmospheric Science, University of Alabama, USA*

'Our analysis of tree rings, ice cores, corals and historical records from around the world indicates that the 1990s were the warmest decade of the millennium.'
*Dr P Jones, University of East Anglia, UK*

### FACT

Some predict that by the 2080s three billion people will suffer from water shortages because of the drier climate.

*Fires can quickly spread after long periods of hot, dry weather. In the Cleveland National Forest in California, USA, firefighters could do little to control the fires which consumed thousands of hectares of forest.*

*In 1998, people in Honduras could only watch as the heavy rains brought by Hurricane Mitch caused the Choluteca river to overflow and flood their homes and businesses.*

## FACT

**In the 1980s, the world's insurers of property lost an average of $2 billion a year from damage claims after extreme weather events. In the 1990s this average had climbed to $12 billion a year.**

## Getting wetter and windier . . .

Global warming may heat up the oceans as well as the land, bringing different climate changes to other areas. A hurricane needs ocean water with temperatures of at least 26 °C to generate the rising warm, moist air that fuels it. With larger areas of warm ocean water the potential for this becomes greater, so global warming may increase the number and intensity of hurricanes, and could also bring these vicious storms to new areas. Hurricanes bring not only strong winds but torrential rainfall too, causing terrible flooding in low-lying areas. In October 1998, Hurricane Mitch dumped the same amount of rain in a week on Central America that would normally fall in a year. Over 10,000 people died in this region from the floods, landslides and 290-kph winds.

However, some believe that there have actually been fewer hurricanes reaching land in the last 50 years. Instead, the problem may lie in the increased number of people who choose to live in coastal areas that are at risk from hurricanes. One example of this is in the Indian state of Orissa. In November 1999, two cyclones hit India's eastern coastline. The second one sucked up the water from the Bay of Bengal into a wall of water 6 m high, submerging villages and flooding the countryside as far as 20 km inland. In all, 9,504 people died, while another 15 million people had to try to piece together their lives after this catastrophe.

The actions of people are also blamed for worsening the flood damage from a hurricane. These actions include building on flood plains, which prevents rainfall from being absorbed into the land, and cutting down trees. We may think that there are more hurricanes because we hear more about them in the media nowadays. After all, damage caused by a hurricane is a dramatic news story for TV and the newspapers.

## VIEWPOINTS

'Some of these floods, droughts and extended heatwaves are quite likely associated with global warming. Indeed in a warmer world we would expect more of these particular types of events.'
Dr Bob Watson, Chairman of the IPCC

'We don't see, at this point, a link between global warming and tropical cyclone activity.'
Dr James Baker, National Oceanic and Atmospheric Administration, USA, May 2000

People in Orissa, India, clutch belongings saved from their flooded homes after the devastating cyclone of November 1999.

### Bigger and stronger El Niño . . .

Scientists are also showing concern over the effects of El Niño and La Niña – the ENSO – which seem to be getting worse. This may be because the effect

of warm ocean water in an El Niño year is combined with, and exaggerated by, the more long-term effects of global warming. The 1997–98 El Niño was the strongest ever recorded, and developed faster than any previous El Niño. During this time, as the warm water remained on the eastern side of the Pacific, rising, moist air brought heavy rainfall and flooding conditions. Parts of Peru suffered rainfall that was ten times the average, causing flooding, mudslides and the loss of lives, homes and food supplies. Rain was even experienced in the coastal desert of Atacama, which is unheard of in normal years.

*Tens of thousands of people in Peru were left homeless and stranded in January 1998 after the heavy rains caused by El Niño triggered mudslides and flash floods.*

Meanwhile, on the western side of the ocean, drought affected the rainforests of Indonesia and the wheat fields of Australia. People living in Melbourne were horrified to see enormous clouds of dust blowing across this Australian city as the land was baked dry and eroded soil was picked up by wind. The drought swept further west across southern India, Sri Lanka and right over to southern Africa as the trade winds across the Indian Ocean failed to drag with them warm, wet conditions as well.

### FACT

96 per cent of all deaths from natural disasters such as floods and droughts occur in developing countries.

### Winners and losers

The 1997–98 El Niño was so powerful that areas alongside other oceans also experienced very unusual, destructive weather. However, some people actually benefited from the 1997–98 El Niño. According to some, the American public saved $6.7 billion on heating bills, and $6.9 billion less was spent on repairs and the clearing-up operations normally necessary after floods from melting snow. In addition no hurricanes came in from the Atlantic Ocean.

Developed countries, such as the USA, have the technology to predict and warn people of extreme weather, and prepare people before a hurricane. In contrast, it is nearly always the poorer countries of the world that are worst affected by these extreme weather events. In total, the 1997–98 El Niño claimed the lives of 21,000 people as a result of the natural disasters that it brought, and most of these deaths were in the developing world. Poorer people are more likely to live in houses made of flimsy materials that are easily destroyed by wind and rain if a major storm hits. When the storm has passed, the poor do not have an insurance policy to pay for damage to their homes or for treatment in hospital.

*Poor villagers in Orissa, India, gaze helplessly at their destroyed home after the 1999 cyclone.*

## VIEWPOINTS

'This El Niño (1997–98) gives us a taste of the extreme, erratic weather our children and grandchildren can expect more of unless we reverse the trend in global warming.'
*Former US Vice President Al Gore*

'El Niños were ignored for decades and are now blamed for everything. That makes it very difficult to measure their true impact.'
*Claude de Ville de Goyet, top official of the Pan-American Health Organization*

**FACT**

1998 was the warmest year of the warmest decade of the warmest century of the millennium.

| 1998: A record-breaking year | |
| --- | --- |
| May 1998 | Mexico suffered its worst drought in 70 years. |
| June 1998 | Heatwaves in northern India killed 4,000 people. |
| September 1998 | Floods in China left 14 million people homeless. |
| Sept/Oct 1998 | Bangladesh experienced its worst floods ever, leaving 30 million people homeless. |
| Oct/Nov 1998 | Over 10,000 people died after Hurricane Mitch swept Central America. |

### Is it all true?

The IPCC claim that the record-setting weather events of 1998 already provide evidence of the effect of climate change on the world's weather, and they predict that worse is yet to come. But can we trust these gloomy forecasts, or are they just good ingredients for a newspaper story? The predictions made by the IPCC are in fact hotly debated as other scientists have questioned the basis of their ideas. Some argue that the IPCC are basing their claims for hotter temperatures on measurements taken from meteorological stations on the edges of towns and cities. As urban areas release their own heat from buildings, factories and vehicles to form a 'heat island', this is bound to influence local temperatures.

Some argue that the IPCC put too much faith in computer models to predict future weather

**VIEWPOINT**

'El Niño does bring some good news. In 1998, we enjoyed magnificent sunsets because of all the dust in the atmosphere blown up from the parched land of Australia.'
*Denis Courtenay, resident of Auckland, New Zealand*

patterns. Despite the development of buoys, research ships and satellites, we still do not have detailed information on the past behaviour of our oceans. Consequently, computer models can only give a simplified version of the real climate, and fail to explain all the complicated relationships between the different pieces of the atmosphere jigsaw. For instance, no one quite knows what knock-on effects the changes in temperature will have on the behaviour of the oceans, and how this will affect wind and cloud cover patterns which could block out some of the Sun's heat.

Given these uncertainties, can we reliably predict the weather of the future?

*In 1998, reservoirs in Mexico ran dry as the country experienced its worst drought for 70 years.*

## DEBATE

Do you think richer countries should help the countries that are most likely to be affected by these more extreme weather events? If so, in what ways should they help?

# RISING SEA LEVELS

## Melting ice

*Some scientists believe that rising temperatures in Antarctica are causing parts of the ice shelves to break up. Others believe that local conditions, like shifts in ocean currents, may be the reason for this, and not global warming.*

If the IPCC's predictions for rising global temperatures are right, the low-lying parts of the world may have another problem to worry about as warmer ocean water melts the polar ice. In 1998, scientists looked at satellite photographs of Antarctica with alarm. It seems that the Larsen B ice shelf, a vast block of ice covering about 150 sq km of ocean, is breaking up and melting. The Larsen B ice shelf has developed over 10,000 years and sticks out from Antarctica's most northern, warmest tip. Since the 1940s, temperatures here have increased by 2.5 °C, and the Larsen B has already lost one-seventh of its area.

A similar picture is developing around the Arctic ice cap. Here, the average thickness of the ice is half what it was 30 years ago and, according to the Worldwatch Institute's report in 2000, it is already shrinking at the rate of 24,000 sq km a year. Land-based ice is also disappearing at a rate of one metre a year across Greenland, which holds 8 per cent of the world's ice. Meanwhile glaciers, from the Alps to the Canadian Rockies to the Himalayas, are shrinking in size. As the ice has melted, humans and animals frozen in ice over 12,000 years ago have been discovered.

*The tusks of a woolly mammoth: in 1998, melting ice in central Siberia
exposed the carcass of a woolly mammoth that lived there 50,000 years ago.*

Until recently, many people jumped to the
conclusion that more melting ice would
automatically mean that sea levels would rise to
new dangerous levels. Some even predicted sea
level rises of up to five or six metres, but are these
claims wildly exaggerated? When you fill a cup
with water and ice, the cup does not overflow
when the ice melts. This is because ice is made up
of very few water particles – the rest is trapped air.
In the same way, large floating icebergs that break
off from polar ice shelves should have little effect
on sea levels as they melt. However, scientists are
generally agreed that if temperatures do become
warmer, the volume of ocean water will expand.
This process of 'thermal expansion' could lead to
higher sea levels, although nothing on the scale
originally predicted.

## VIEWPOINTS

'Our ancestors are
emerging from the ice
with a message for us:
the Earth is getting
warmer.'
*Lester Brown, President of
the Worldwatch Institute*

'Whether or not
changes in the climate
in Antarctica are a
direct result of man's
influence is still an
open question.'
*Dr David Vaughn, British
Antarctic Survey*

## VIEWPOINT

'The greenhouse effect and sea level rise threaten the very heart of our existence.'
*Prime Minister of Tuvalu at the World Climate Conference, November 1990*

## Danger to people on the low lands

The IPCC claim that there has already been a 15-cm rise in sea levels in the last 100 years, and there could be a further rise of 18 cm by 2030. Half the world's population lives in low-lying coastal zones which include many large cities, such as New York, London, Bangkok and Tokyo. This suggests that even small sea-level rises could affect the lives of many people. This is particularly true for people who live just above sea level.

The South Pacific islands of Kiribati and Tuvalu are less than 4 m above sea level. Studies show that sea levels here are already rising at 1.5 mm a year, and Kiribati has already had coastal roads washed away by the sea in recent years. By the end of this century, the coast may retreat by tens of metres, and eventually the inhabitants of these islands may have to give up their homes entirely and move elsewhere. Although other South Pacific islands like Fiji have higher ground, most people live along the coastline where it is easier to make a living from fishing, tourism and growing sugar cane on the flat coastal plains. All this may be at risk in the future.

*Cities that lie on the coast, like New York, are likely to be badly affected if sea levels rise.*

## Flooding from two sides in Bangladesh

Bangladesh is another country which is especially at risk from flooding. The coast of this densely populated country is so low that even a tiny rise in sea level could be catastrophic. Most of Bangladesh is situated in a flat, low-lying delta criss-crossed by the rivers Ganges, Brahmaputra and Meghna. These flood the land every July and August after heavy rains in the Himalayas have fed the rivers. As a result, the country can be flooded in two different ways. Although Bangladesh relies on river flooding to fertilize the land naturally with sediments, floods in recent years have been much greater and have lasted longer, putting many people's lives at risk.

The Bangladesh floods in 1998 were by far the worst on record. The causes of these floods are complex, but in part scientists blame the extra-heavy rain in the Himalayas which meant that the rivers were especially high, as well as a rise in sea level in the Bay of Bengal. Both of these causes could be a result of climate change.

### VIEWPOINT

'Low-lying countries such as Bangladesh are most vulnerable to the effects of climate change through sea-level rise and the subsequent flooding of agricultural land. Not only does it affect people's livelihoods, but it also leads to population displacement.'
*Dr Peter Newell, Institute of Development Studies, UK*

## Learning from past experiences

Rising sea levels may also threaten much of Holland. Like Bangladesh, Holland lies on a low-lying delta of three major rivers, the Rhine, the Maas and the Scheldt, and the Dutch have already experienced serious flooding from the sea in the past. In February 1953, a vicious storm in the North Sea broke through the sea walls, called dykes, that were designed to protect the land behind them. This tragedy caused the deaths of 1,853 people and the flooding of thousands of square kilometres of valuable farmland. Since then, the Dutch have been determined to improve their protection from the sea so that such a disaster never happens again. To protect settlements and farmland, the Dutch have invested vast amounts of money in 'The Delta Plan' to dam up the openings to the North Sea along the south-west coast of Holland. These massive engineering works involve a series of stronger dykes and a storm surge barrier that automatically closes if the water reaches dangerously high levels.

*In Holland, the Dutch have built a storm surge barrier across the eastern Scheldt river. It acts like an open dam that can be closed when dangerously high water levels are forecast.*

The trouble is that not every country at risk has the same money and expertise as the Dutch to guard against possible floods. Instead, as with extreme weather events, it will be the poorer countries such as Bangladesh and the small island states of the South Pacific that will suffer most if sea levels rise. Although the people of Bangladesh have developed ways to live with the floods, including the setting up of floating shops, and building houses adapted to high water levels, life may be more difficult in the

## VIEWPOINT

'Few farmers could farm land under sea level without having to worry. Fortunately, the Dutch engineers have made it possible here in the Netherlands. No one expects a repeat of the flooding of February 1953; we can farm here in complete confidence.'
*Wouter Galle, Dutch farmer*

future if their annual floods become ever bigger and last longer. Many of the 125 million people who live in Bangladesh have nowhere else to go. In the world today, there are already 25 million people who have been forced to leave their homes as a result of natural disasters such as droughts and floods. Could this be the beginning of a huge wave of environmental refugees, forced to move elsewhere due to climate change?

## FACT

By the 2080s, it is predicted that higher sea levels will flood 94 million people a year compared to 13 million people today.

*During September 1998, three-quarters of Bangladesh was submerged by flood water. Nearly 1,000 people died and the lives of 30 million others were affected.*

*In 1990 IPCC scientists made the following predictions about global rises in sea level. The diagram shows three possible outcomes:*

**A** *If we increase world greenhouse gas emissions*

**B** *If we continue to release similar amounts as we do now*

**C** *If we cut emissions by changing the way we live now*

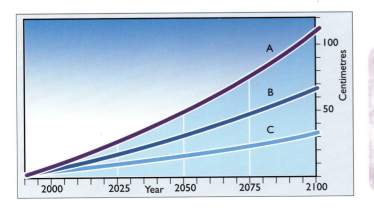

## DEBATE

Do you think that people living in low-lying areas should pay extra insurance because of the higher risks of damage to their property?

# WARNING SIGNS FROM THE NATURAL WORLD

*Plant and animal species in Costa Rica's cloud forests are specially adapted to the damp, misty conditions found there.*

## Strange behaviour

All species in the natural environment adapt to fluctuations in the climate. However, more and more evidence suggests that plants and animals in different climatic zones have been changing their habits in response to the extreme weather events of recent years. Some ecologists studying seasonal climates, for example in north-west Europe, believe that spring starts 18 days earlier today than it did in 1900, causing animals to behave differently. Birds have continued to sing throughout the winter, and some species of butterfly have been spotted in areas where they have never been seen before. Is this just part of the natural long-term cycle of adaptation, or are plant and animal species struggling to keep up with accelerated climate change?

### Casualties in the cloud forest

Signs of the natural world under stress from climate change have been observed among species that inhabit tropical rainforests, the richest and most diverse ecosystems on Earth. In the rainforests of Costa Rica, animals and plants have adapted to particular levels of altitude. The higher levels are often enveloped in a blanket of water vapour that has evaporated from the warm waters of the Caribbean Sea. The 'cloud forest' that develops from this supply of water vapour has its own characteristic species that thrive in this wet, mossy environment. If global temperatures rise, it is possible that instead of hanging over the forest, the water vapour will be lifted higher up, denying the forest its moisture.

Already, studies of Costa Rica's cloud forests show a greater number of uncharacteristically dry periods and changes in the type of species that inhabit these areas. The golden toad, a resident of the cloud forests, has not been seen since the 1980s. Scientists are guessing that it may have been wiped out by fungal diseases spread by the higher temperatures. It is also possible that water temperatures in the forest's rivers and pools have become too warm for the golden toad. What is worse is that it may not be the only victim of climate change in these lush cloud forests.

## VIEWPOINT

'The golden toad may become known as the first species whose extinction is attributed to recent global warming. The amphibian declines are part of a suite of changes that have affected reptiles and birds as well as frogs, toads and salamanders.'
*Dr Alan Pounds, ecologist, Costa Rica*

*Male golden toads in the Monteverde Cloud Forest in Costa Rica. As they have not been seen since the 1980s, it is feared golden toads are now extinct.*

*Coral reefs are very delicate environments as they are sensitive to even small changes in water temperature.*

## FACT

Although coral reefs are found in only 0.2 per cent of the world's oceans, a single reef may contain as many as 3,000 different species of coral, and coral reefs support 25 per cent of all marine fish.

## Coral reefs under threat

Coral is composed of tiny sea creatures called 'coral polyps' that depend on tiny algae that live on their surfaces to provide food. These algae also give the coral their vibrant range of colours. At the same time, the algae are protected by the coral polyps and live off some of the polyps' waste products and carbon dioxide. However, for a coral reef to survive, water temperatures need to be between 21 °C and 30 °C. If the water temperatures exceed 32 °C, the corals are under stress and react by getting rid of the algae. When this happens, the corals turn white, or 'bleach', as they lose their colour. If temperatures return to normal, the corals can recover. However, if temperatures continue to be excessively high over a few weeks, another type of algae takes over that slowly kills the coral.

Other possible side-effects of warmer global temperatures may weaken the reefs still further; rising sea levels may give coral reefs less access to the sunlight they need to grow, and more extreme storms may damage the delicate corals. As a result, this ecosystem, which has built up slowly over thousands of years, can be turned into an underwater wasteland devoid of colour in a matter of weeks.

More and more signs of coral bleaching have been identified right across the tropical oceans in recent years. Even though coral reefs in the Pacific and Indian oceans have withstood the changes in water temperatures of hundreds of El Niños in the past, studies of the effects of the 1997–98 El Niño revealed for the first time that entire coral reefs have been bleached.

## VIEWPOINTS

'Corals have survived historic changes in water temperatures far greater than the current or predicted CO₂-related increases.'
*Dr P J Michaels, editor of 'The World Climate'*

'The havoc global warming could wreak on ocean life may be much greater than we previously imagined.'
*World Wide Fund for Nature representative*

*The destruction of coral reefs through bleaching also destroys the habitat of the many fish that live in this environment.*

## Polar bears under stress

*A mother polar bear plays with her cubs in Hudson Bay, Canada. Warmer temperatures in the far north are shortening the hunting season for polar bears so they are finding it harder to feed their cubs.*

Signs of stress are not limited to tropical regions. Temperatures in the Arctic have warmed faster than most areas in recent decades; and this could be affecting the behaviour of wildlife. Polar bears hunt ringed seals for food by prowling across the ice shelves that cover the sea during the long winters. Hunting is particularly good during April and May when the ice is still thick enough to stand

the weight of a large polar bear and there is a plentiful supply of baby seals for prey. However, warmer temperatures mean that the ice is not as thick as it used to be, and the ice is breaking up earlier, which means the hunting season for the polar bears is shortened. As a result, polar bears are going hungry, and females have less chance of becoming pregnant. Over time, this could lead to a significant fall in the number of polar bears that inhabit these northern climatic zones.

## One change leads to another

In any ecosystem, every plant, animal and insect is linked to other species as part of a web of life. Each species is also dependent on particular conditions of light, temperature, food source and so on. The complex system of inter-relationships between different species means that damage to, or the destruction of, one species may trigger a negative chain reaction that will be felt throughout the ecosystem. This is particularly true of tropical rainforests and coral reefs, which have a vast number of inter-relationships. This makes the whole ecosystem especially vulnerable to even the smallest of changes in climate. The extinction of species such as the golden toad may have damaging effects on the whole rainforest environment which will be impossible to reverse. Meanwhile, if the rich coral reef ecosystems are reduced to rubble, islands will be deprived of their natural protection from stormy seas. The knock-on effects of this on fish populations and the tourism industry may prove disastrous for the people of these areas too.

There is still no proof that recent climate changes are responsible for these disruptions to life on Earth. However, there is a growing amount of evidence from different ecosystems around the world to suggest that it is more than just a coincidence.

## VIEWPOINT

'We are seeing changes in two decades that you wouldn't expect to see in a lifetime. Nature is really confused.'
*Tim Sparks, Institute of Terrestrial Ecology*

## DEBATE

Over 100 countries currently profit by using their coral reefs as tourist attractions. Do you think this should become a thing of the past?

# FEEDING THE WORLD

## Farming and climate change

Climatic conditions have always been the most important influences on people's ability to grow food, and every farming region of the world is adjusted to its own climatic conditions. As with natural ecosystems, many crops are very sensitive to tiny changes in temperature and water supply; a frost in southern Brazil can wipe out the region's coffee harvest for the year. Already, millions of people are forced to farm in difficult environments known as marginal areas. If the global climate system changes and natural environments shift location, will we be able to grow enough food to feed the world's population in the future?

### Flooded food

The rice-growing calendar in Southeast Asia is adjusted to the changes in the climate during the course of the year. The monsoon rains provide the rice paddies with natural irrigation while the drier sunny months help to ripen the rice crop in time for harvest. If this climate pattern changes, the rice harvests which have fed people for thousands of years may be at risk. In parts of Asia, higher temperatures and evaporation of water may leave the rice plants without the water they need to grow, and cause a drop of 20 per cent in the annual rice harvest.

*Harvesting coffee beans on plantations in southern Brazil supports thousands of people. A frost could wipe out the entire coffee harvest for a year.*

*Across the 'rice bowl' of South-east Asia, planting and harvesting rice
is timed according to the seasonal changes in the climate.*

At the same time, the low-lying rice paddies of
Bangladesh may receive excessive rainfall.
Permanent flooding of these fertile lands would
cause the rice plants to rot and die, leaving the
country's 125 million people without their most
important food crop.

## Trouble at sea
People who rely on fish from the sea as a source of
food may be at risk too. During El Niño years,
fishing communities along the coast of South
America have suffered a massive reduction in fish
catches because the warm water that sits along the
eastern Pacific forces fish to move to cooler waters
to the north, or to dive deeper to cooler ocean
depths. During the 1997–98 El Niño, Peruvian
fishermen sat idle along the coast, and the pelicans
that benefited from the fish died. Smaller fish
catches also reduced the amount of fishmeal
available to feed poultry and livestock.

## VIEWPOINTS

'By the 2050s climate
change alone is
forecast to put an
extra 30 million people
at risk of hunger.'
*UK Meteorological Office*

'As the planet warms,
winters become less
severe, growing seasons
become longer, and more
food than ever is
produced as the planet
becomes greener.'
*Professor P J Michaels,
Environmental Sciences
Department, University of
Virginia, USA*

## VIEWPOINT

'My cotton and wheat fields all dried up in the year of 1988. The rains just never came. I reckon it's because of all this global warming.'
*Esker Cotton, north-central Texas, USA*

## Drought, soil erosion and food shortages

Climate changes elsewhere may lead to drought. Already, one-third of the Earth's land surface, home to 600 million people, receives less than 600 mm of rainfall a year. With higher temperatures and even less rain, soils can dry out and, baked by the Sun, become fine and dusty. Winds can easily erode this valuable topsoil and, once lost, the land can become degraded, making it difficult to grow crops. With longer and more frequent droughts, food production in the wheat-growing fields of the North American prairies, known as the breadbasket of the world, could fall dramatically. In 1988, severe drought in these productive lands turned many fields into dustbowls, and poor harvests meant that world grain reserves dropped to a record low of just 60 days. Perhaps this should be a warning for the future.

*Children queuing to receive food rations in Sudan. More frequent droughts will make this situation more common and more widespread.*

The situation could be even more serious in poorer parts of the world that already experience low, unreliable levels of rainfall. Here, land degradation could prove catastrophic to millions of people. Famines, such as that in the Horn of Africa in

2000, could become a much more common occurrence, forcing many people to leave their homes and move in search of food.

## Simple but successful solutions to fight drought

However, people have managed to adjust to changing climatic conditions in the past, and perhaps changes in the way we farm and manage the land may be the answer to avoid catastrophe. People in poorer countries often have to rely on local knowledge and local resources to fight the effects of drought. By adjusting cropping patterns

*In Burkina Faso, small stone walls built across the land slopes trap water as it flows downhill. This way, water trickles out gradually between the gaps in the stones and stops the valuable topsoil from being washed away.*

and by making more efficient use of water with better irrigation systems, food production in drier climates could be more successful. In areas of the Sahel, a belt of dry land that stretches across Africa on the southern edge of the Sahara desert, people have developed imaginative ways to produce enough food from these marginal lands. By creating small stone walls to hold back the soil and water after rain, and creating windbreaks from trees, the people of Yatenga province in northern Burkina Faso have managed to improve their crop harvests.

## Is biotechnology the answer?

Richer countries can use technology to fight land degradation. Fertilizers can help to make the soil productive again. It is now possible to grow crops in completely artificial environments where people can adjust the temperature and water supply to maximize the harvest. In Holland, vegetables are sometimes grown hydroponically (suspended in water). There is also a lot of new research in biotechnology, which uses laboratory testing to develop new strains of crop. Scientists have already developed new crop varieties that are resistant to drought, pests and diseases, and there is now more success in the genetic modification of plants – taking one gene and adding it to another plant. However, this technology is expensive, and there are still questions that remain over its possible risk to human health, and no scientist can know for sure what effect these genetically-modified plants will have on the natural workings of an ecosystem.

*At the Epcot Center in Florida, USA, technology is being used to grow plants hydroponically, in nutrient-rich water instead of in soil.*

## New food frontiers

There is also a possibility that while climate changes may reduce food production in some areas, other difficult, marginal environments may become more suitable for food production. In the long-term, increases in rainfall in some parts of South-east Asia, such as western Java, may extend the area of rice farming, and warmer winters in Siberia may create a new productive wheat-growing region.

Some scientists believe that greater concentrations of $CO_2$ in our atmosphere may also have a positive effect on food production, as the gas promotes biological productivity. With higher concentrations of $CO_2$, plants make better use of their water supply and can cope with drought more easily. Scientists working for the Western Fuels Association predict a 30–60 per cent increase in harvests of soy beans, wheat and other crops if $CO_2$ levels increase.

*Thanks to warmer temperatures, wheat farmers in Australia are enjoying better harvests as frosts have become less common.*

## DEBATE

Biotechnology could change the way in which we produce food in the future as companies develop new genetically-modified crops. Should this technology be supplied free to all those that need it?

# CLIMATE CHANGE AND HUMAN HEALTH

*People keeping cool during a heatwave. Scientists predict that sweltering heatwaves with temperatures above 33 °C could increase the number of deaths from heatstroke tenfold.*

## Seasonal sickness

If predictions for more extreme temperatures prove true, people living in seasonal climates may benefit from fewer outbreaks of flu during the winter as temperatures become warmer. However, during the summer months more people could suffer from allergic diseases like asthma and hay fever, as pollen-producing plants thrive in the warmth. More serious effects include the possible fatal heatstrokes caused by hot weather.

## Choking smoke

Extreme weather events may bring health risks indirectly as air quality declines and bugs and diseases are given new opportunities to spread.

*Across South-east Asia in September 1997, people had to wear face masks to filter the smoke-filled air as Indonesia's forests burnt out of control.*

The drought in Indonesia, caused by the 1997–98 El Niño, meant that forest fires started by farmers to clear land burnt out of control as there was no rain to put them out. The enormous amounts of smoke from these fires filled the atmosphere and spread right across the region. In the cities of Malaysia, the air quality was so bad that many people found it difficult to breathe. The hospitals were full of people with respiratory diseases, and schools were closed for weeks.

## Water-borne diseases

After a drought, a flood or a hurricane, clean water may be difficult to find. As a result, people may be forced to drink water that is contaminated with sewage and other pollutants. Water-borne diseases, such as diarrhoea and cholera, can all thrive in contaminated water. When a person catches one of these water-borne diseases, they can lose large amounts of body fluid, including essential salts, which can lead to severe dehydration. Without access to clean water to replace these lost fluids people can die.

## VIEWPOINTS

'At present, most of the US population is protected against the adverse health outcomes associated with weather and/or climate.'
*Dr J A Patz, School of Public Health, John Hopkins University, USA*

'As we continue to disrupt ecosystems through a variety of mechanisms, including changing the Earth's climate, we can anticipate that new diseases and health threats will result.'
*J Balbus, Chairman of George Washington University School of Public Health & Health Services, USA*

## FACT

During the warm months of 1998, there were more than 475,000 cases of dengue fever in Brazil, more than in the whole of South America in previous years.

## The mosquito menace

Perhaps the most worrying effect climate changes may have on our health is from changes in the life cycles of insects that carry diseases – particularly certain types of mosquito. In recent years, doctors and health workers have noticed more cases of other infectious diseases carried by mosquitoes in tropical areas. The spread of dengue fever, passed on by the female *aedes* mosquito, poses a threat to human health. This disease has been nicknamed, 'the breaking bones fever' because it causes blinding headaches, severe muscle and joint pains and even death.

*To keep healthy during the 1998 floods in Bangladesh, people had to wade or swim through dirty flood water to collect clean water from communal water taps.*

Dengue fever used to be limited to areas up to 1,000 m above sea level, but with higher temperatures in the hills and mountains, dengue fever has spread into regions of India and Colombia up to 2,200 m above sea level.

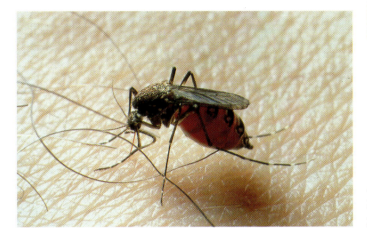

*A female mosquito sucks blood from a human arm. Mosquitoes need the blood to feed their eggs.*

## The spread of malaria

Mosquitoes can also carry malarial parasites. These parasites are spread most successfully when temperatures are above 16 °C, which speeds up their life cycle. Malaria is spread when a female *anopheles* mosquito carrying a tiny parasite bites through a person's skin and passes on the parasite in its saliva. If another female *anopheles* mosquito bites someone infected by malaria, it will pick up the parasite from the person's blood. It will then pass on the disease to somebody else. If a lot of people catch the disease in one area, it is called an epidemic.

Most cases of malaria infection today are found in warm, wet regions where heavy rain can create puddles in which the mosquitoes breed. Once infected, a person will develop a high fever and will have to lie in bed seriously ill for weeks. One type of malaria affects the brain and can kill a person in a matter of days.

## VIEWPOINTS

'Malaria is today a developing country issue. With climate change, it could become a problem for developed countries too.'
*Philippe Martin, EC Joint Research Centre*

'I don't believe climate is driving the malaria epidemic at present. It has more to do with failing health services, resistance to drugs and ecology.'
*Steve Lindsay, malaria specialist, University of Durham, UK*

**FACT**

Shakespeare referred to the ague (malaria) in several of his plays, for example, *The Tempest*.

Today, more than 300 million people suffer from malaria and one million people die from the disease each year. Some people believe that there could be an extra 620 million victims a year by 2050, as warmer, wetter weather could see the malarial mosquito moving to new areas. With warmer temperatures, North America and Europe may have to face the threat of malaria too.

### The 'ague' of the Middle Ages

What is confusing is that looking back in history, areas with much colder temperatures have also suffered malaria epidemics. Between 1550–1770, the UK had a little ice age, when temperatures fell by one or two degrees. At this time, malaria, or 'the ague' as it was known, was widespread, especially in marshy areas where mosquitoes can breed easily.

*Irrigation canals have improved life for millions in drier parts of the world, but they have also created new health risks.*

Oliver Cromwell, ruler of England for almost ten years, died of the ague in 1658. In the eighteenth and early nineteenth centuries, malaria could be found throughout North America too. This has encouraged some scientists to question the link between the spread of malaria and climate change.

## Malaria prevention and treatment

Instead of climate change, some scientists believe that creating the conditions in which mosquitoes breed is more responsible for the spread of the disease. In Europe and North America, many of the marshes that used to be home to the malarial mosquito have been drained to create new farmland, and chemicals are sprayed on the land to kill pests and diseases, including mosquitoes. Meanwhile, in many developing countries, open sewers and irrigation canals that are built to water crops in drier areas have increased the breeding grounds of the *anopheles* mosquito. At the same time, health services in poorer countries may not have enough medicines to treat people who catch malaria. Cleaner water, proper sewage facilities, better housing and medical services could all help to reduce the spread of malaria. Therefore, getting rid of poverty may be more important than tackling climate change in the battle against malaria.

## Prepare for new risks

Pests and diseases can adapt to new conditions and develop a resistance to the drugs designed to kill them. It is possible that we may have to experience completely new health threats as pests and diseases respond to changes in the Earth's climate. Scientists today can only guess the future effects of climate change on human health because the data collected in the past does not give them enough information to be certain of the future. In the meantime, it may be better to improve living conditions in areas where diseases can easily spread.

## DEBATE

Scientists have had to develop stronger and stronger medicines to protect people from the threat of malaria as mosquitoes develop resistance to these drugs. Should we come to expect more illness and death as the climate changes, or should more money be spent on medical research so that science can continue to stay one step ahead?

# INTERNATIONAL CO-OPERATION

## Global solutions to global problems

Predicting accurate changes in our climate is difficult. Although scientists today recognize that human activity is adding to the layer of gases in our atmosphere, they cannot agree on whether our contribution to these gases really makes a difference to global temperatures. Computer models used to forecast long-term climate change are unlikely to be accurate because the climate system is so complicated. Also, despite today's technology, scientists continue to disagree about the possible future effects of global warming. Nevertheless, wherever or whoever produces the greenhouse gases, the effect that this may have on the climate will be global. It is important therefore that individual countries come together to make agreements on greenhouse gas emissions.

*A flooded supermarket in England. In 2000, England and Wales suffered the worst flooding for 50 years and the wettest autumn since 1766, when records began. Was this the result of global warming?*

## Better to be safe than sorry

In light of these uncertainties, some people argue that we should wait until we are sure of the effects of human activity on our climate. However, many other scientists and environmentalists argue that doing nothing now could put great risks to life on Earth in the future, and that we should not wait for disasters to happen. Instead, perhaps we should respond to the growing amount of scientific evidence on the possible effects of climate change. Just in case, we should take action to reduce the amount of greenhouse gases we are adding to the atmosphere. This is called the 'precautionary principle'.

## Changing energy use

Some countries have been taking the 'precautionary principle' seriously and have begun to reduce the amount of greenhouse gases that are released through human activity, particularly $CO_2$, the main greenhouse gas. By developing cleaner ways of making energy, we can reduce the amount of $CO_2$. New gas turbine power stations release half the amount of $CO_2$ compared to old fashioned coal-fired power stations. They are also more efficient as much less of the energy in a gas turbine power station is lost through escaped heat. Using alternative energy sources to fossil fuels is even better because they do not release $CO_2$ at all. In the future, more of our energy could come from wind farms and solar power. Unlike fossil fuels, the Sun and wind are renewable sources of energy that will not run out.

*Wind farms provide energy without producing $CO_2$ but, like this wind farm in California, USA, they take up huge areas of land to generate enough energy.*

## FACT

Norway gets rid of waste $CO_2$ by freezing it and injecting it into the sandstone beneath the ocean floor.

*In Costa Rica the environmental group Arbofolia is planting trees to restore the original environment. Tree planting is a simple and cheap way of absorbing the $CO_2$ that might contribute to climate change.*

## VIEWPOINT

'Increasing the fuel efficiency of automobiles is the biggest single step that could be taken by the US government.'
*Dan Becker, spokesperson for the US environmental Sierra Club*

### Energy efficiency

There are also opportunities for us to use energy more efficiently. In cold climates we can insulate buildings so that less heat is lost and save on the amount of energy we use. Car companies are now developing better engines that run on less fuel than older models, and new technologies in home appliances, such as washing machines and refrigerators, are more energy efficient. These are some of the ways we can reduce the amount of $CO_2$ and other greenhouse gases that we add to the atmosphere.

Controlling deforestation and tree planting could help as well, as more trees can also reduce the $CO_2$ in the atmosphere. Norway has even managed to cut its $CO_2$ emissions by 3 per cent by freezing the gas and then pumping it into underlying rock. In the future these $CO_2$ dumps could be important for many countries.

## Expensive technology

Nevertheless, even if every country adopted the 'precautionary principle' we may have to wait a very long time to see the benefits of reducing our greenhouse gas emissions. Many of these measures are expensive too. For a poor country already in debt to international banks, it may be too costly to introduce new energy-efficient technology or to change over its sources of energy to cleaner alternatives.

Modern public transport systems, like the Skytrain in Vancouver, Canada, may encourage more people to leave their cars at home. This will help to reduce the amount of greenhouse gases that cars add to the atmosphere.

## FACT

Attempts are being made to reduce other greenhouse gas emissions. A North American company, Global Livestock Group, is developing a feed supplement for cattle which helps them digest food more easily. If this works, less methane will be released into the atmosphere!

## VIEWPOINT

'Even if we closed every factory in the world at midnight tonight, there would be enough carbon in the atmosphere to keep it warm for generations.'
Dr M Hulme, climatologist, University of East Anglia, UK

## FACT

Some US experts believe that cuts in carbon dioxide would cost every American $2,000 a year in higher fuel bills.

*Traffic congestion in New York. In the USA the number of vehicles on the roads is increasing every year. In Los Angeles there are already more cars than people.*

## VIEWPOINT

'Climate change is a question of social justice because those who contribute most to the problem are not those who will suffer its worst consequences. This places the onus of responsibility for taking action on the biggest polluters such as the USA.'
Dr Peter Newell, Institute of Development Studies, UK

### The big polluters

Negotiations between countries on these issues are never easy. In many ways, it is like a 'tug of war'. The USA, the world's most powerful industrial nation, relies on fossil fuels to power its industry, and the most common form of transport is the car. About one-quarter of all $CO_2$ emissions come from the USA, even though Americans make up only 4 per cent of the world's population. $CO_2$ levels cannot be reduced without harming the economy because people would have to pay more for their fuel and energy. With higher energy costs, every product made in the USA would cost more to make. Worse still, many people employed in oil- and coal-producing industries might lose their jobs.

In order to fight to keep $CO_2$ emissions as they are, many fossil fuel and transport companies have grouped together to form the Global Climate Coalition, nicknamed 'The Carbon Club'. This organization campaigns fiercely to protect their interests and save jobs in their companies. Meanwhile, there are countries, such as China, that are industrializing fast, and are likely to increase their emissions of greenhouse gases a lot in the years to come. Within ten years from now, it is likely that China will overtake the USA as the world's biggest producer of $CO_2$.

## The victims of climate change

Poorer countries like Bangladesh and the island states of the South Pacific are in a very different bargaining position. While their contribution to the total of greenhouse gases is very small they have already borne the brunt of the extreme weather, food shortages and rises in sea level, and in the future they may lose their homelands altogether. At the same time, two billion people in poorer countries still do not have electricity. Consequently, many people have questioned whether it is fair for a poor country to make the same cuts in $CO_2$ as a richer country. After all, it is the industries of the developed world that have been most responsible for greenhouse gas emissions in the past.

## VIEWPOINTS

'Growth in emissions by developing countries will account for the majority of future emissions. So without participation by developing countries international treaties are unlikely to be effective and fair.'
*B P Flannery, Science Strategy and Programs Manager, Exxon Mobil Corporation*

'In the developed world, only two people ride in a car and you want us to give up riding the bus!'
*Zhong Shukong, Chinese representative at Kyoto conference*

*Bicycles and buses at rush hour in Beijing. As Chinese people become richer, they may choose to replace their bicycles with cars or motorbikes, adding to the greenhouse gases in the atmosphere.*

## World leaders reach agreement in Kyoto

To show international co-operation, world leaders met in Kyoto, Japan, in December 1997 to try to agree on targets for cuts in greenhouse gas emissions. After days of debate, 83 countries signed an agreement that became known as the Kyoto Protocol. They agreed to reduce average $CO_2$ emissions by 5.2 per cent of 1990's levels by the year 2010. President Clinton agreed to cuts of 7 per cent in the USA, and European countries went further still, agreeing to cuts of 8 per cent. For the time being, developing countries did not have to make cuts in their greenhouse gas emissions.

## Trading pollution

Agreements like the Kyoto Protocol mean little unless governments actually take action. The problem is that the agreement can only be enforced once 60 countries have made the agreement part of their own national law, or 'ratified' it. Sadly, only 14 countries have since ratified the Kyoto Protocol. The Kyoto Protocol also permitted richer countries to 'buy' the $CO_2$ allowances of other countries through a system of 'tradeable permits'. In this way, it is possible that many of the biggest polluters will not have to make any cuts at all.

*Jan Pronk, Dutch Chairman of the November 2000 Climate Change conference in The Hague, adds the final sandbag to a 1.5 m-high wall of sandbags. Protesters built this wall to draw attention to the floods that people may face if world leaders cannot reach an agreement on greenhouse gas cuts.*

**VIEWPOINT**

'I'm disappointed, but this is not the end.'
*Michael Meacher, UK representative after The Hague Conference*

*The failure of many countries to ratify the Kyoto Protocol of 1997, and the lack of any agreement in The Hague in 2000, suggests that there will be little change in the emission of greenhouse gases from power stations and other sources in the near future.*

## No agreement in The Hague

Representatives from 180 countries met again in The Hague, Holland, in November 2000. Despite a whole week of talking, arguing and negotiating late into the night, they left the conference without any agreement that would build on the Kyoto Protocol.

## Too little, too late?

After the failure of the Hague Conference, it remains to be seen whether the Kyoto Protocol will really change the habits of any of the countries that signed the agreement. Nevertheless, the agreement shows that every country in the world has an interest in climate change, and the Kyoto Protocol may mark a turning point in the way we use our planet to ensure life on Earth for future generations.

**DEBATE**

Should poorer countries be forced to stick within fixed limits of gas emissions or should they be given the opportunity to develop their economies in the same way that developed countries have in the past?

# GLOSSARY

**algae**  types of microscopic plant that grow in water.

**allergic disease**  an illness caused by the body's reaction to something breathed in, eaten or drunk.

**anemometer**  an instrument used for measuring wind speed.

**atmosphere**  the mixture of gases that form a 'blanket' around the Earth.

**barometer**  an instrument used for measuring air pressure in the atmosphere.

**buoy**  a floating vessel that can store weather equipment and guide ships in dangerous waters.

**CFCs**  short for chlorofluorocarbons, a group of gases including fluorine, chlorine and carbon that have been used in the manufacture of various products, e.g. refrigerators, cleaning solvents and plastic foams.

**climate**  the average weather conditions for a place taken over a period of time.

**cyclone**  a severe tropical storm that can build up in a tropical ocean, bringing heavy rain and very strong winds.

**deforestation**  the clearance of trees from the land.

**degradation**  describes land that has lost its long-term ability to produce food crops.

**delta**  a triangular area of flat land at the mouth of a river, made up of silt deposited by the river as it enters the sea or a lake.

**ecosystem**  a natural system of plants and animals where species interact with each other and with the non-living environment of the climate, soil and rock.

**eroded**  worn away by the movement of running water, glaciers or the wind.

**famine**  an extreme shortage of food over a long period of time. Poorer people may starve to death because they cannot grow or buy enough food.

**fossil fuels**  types of energy sources, such as coal, oil and gas, that are formed from fossilized plants and animals. They release carbon when they are burned.

**Gulf Stream**  a warm ocean current that strongly influences the climate of north-west Europe.

**hemisphere**  the two halves of the Earth, divided by the Equator. The northern hemisphere is above the Equator and the southern hemisphere below it.

**humidity**  a measure of how much moisture the air contains.

**Industrial Revolution**  the period in the late eighteenth and early nineteenth centuries (150–200 years ago) when new machinery and the use of fossil fuels to generate energy led to the start of modern industry and dramatic changes in the way people lived.

**irrigation**  methods of artificially watering the land, using water from rivers and wells, to help crops grow.

**latitude (lines of)**  imaginary horizontal lines which circle the Earth. They show how far north or south from the Equator a place is.

**meteorologist**  a person who studies the science of weather and climate, especially weather forecasting.

**natural disaster**  an extreme natural event that causes damage to people and property, such as a drought, flood, hurricane or volcanic eruption.

**orbit**  to travel in a circle around an object. The Earth orbits the Sun once a year.

**parasite** an organism that lives off another organism.

**prairies** large areas of grassland, often used for growing crops or rearing animals.

**precipitation** all forms of water that fall from the sky onto the land, such as rain, snow, hail, sleet, dew, frost or fog.

**respiration** the way in which an organism takes in and absorbs oxygen when breathing in, and releases carbon dioxide when breathing out.

**respiratory disease** an illness that affects a person's lungs so they have difficulty in breathing normally.

**rice paddy** wet land in which rice is grown.

**trade winds** reliable winds in both the northern and southern hemispheres that blow into the area of low pressure around the Equator. Their direction is influenced by the Earth's rotation.

**tropical rainforest** the natural type of vegetation that grows in an equatorial climate. Over one-third of the world's trees grow in tropical rainforests.

**weather** the day-to-day condition of the atmosphere, e.g. the temperature, cloudiness and rainfall affecting a particular place.

# BOOKS AND CD-ROMS

## BOOKS TO READ

**Climate Change: What's Happening to the Weather?** Richard Buckley (Understanding Global Issues, 1997)

**The Earth Strikes Back: Water** Pamela Grant and Arthur Haswell (Belitha, 1999)

**Energy and Climate Change** (WWF-UK, 1997)

**Energy and Resources** Paul Brown (Franklin Watts, 1998)

**Energy Matters** Centre for Sustainable Energy (CSE Bristol, 1999)

**Floods** (Restless Planet series) Emma Durham and Mark Maslin (Wayland, 1999)

**The Greenhouse Effect** Alex Edmonds (Watts, 1996)

**Keeping the Air Clean** John Baines (Wayland, 1997)

**Repairing the Damage: Fires and Floods** David Lambert (Evans, 1997)

**Restless Earth: Floods and Tidal Waves** Terry Jennings (Belitha, 1999)

**Storms** (Restless Planet series) Mark Maslin (Wayland, 1999)

**Weird Weather** Paul Simons (Warner Books, 1997)

## CD-ROMS

**Interfact: Weather** (Worldaware, 1999) PC and Mac versions available. Looks at the water cycle, wind, snow, droughts, floods and the seasons.

**In the Eye of the Storm** (Action Aid, 1999) PC and Mac versions available. Interactive CD including video clips, satellite images and photos, looking at the effect of a cyclone on a Bangladeshi community.

# ADDRESSES

## ADDRESSES

**Centre for Alternative Technology**
Llwyngwern Quarry
Machynlleth
Powys SY20 9AZ
Tel: 01654 702400

**Friends of the Earth**
26-28 Underwood Street
London N1 7JQ
Tel: 020 7490 1555

**Global Action Plan**
8 Fulwood Place
London WC1V 6HG
Tel: 020 7405 5633

**Greenpeace UK**
Canonbury Villas
London N1 2PN
Tel: 020 7865 8100

**The Meteorological Office**
London Road
Bracknell
Berkshire RG12 2SY
Tel: 0845 300 0300

**Reforest the Earth**
48 Bethel Street
Norwich
Norfolk NR2 1NR
Tel: 01603 631007

## WEB SITES

**Athena Curriculum**: explains the mechanics of El Niño.
http://athena.wednet.edu/curric/oceans/elnino/

**BBC**: a general site on the impact of climate change on natural ecosystems.
www.bbc.co.uk/nature/earth/warnings

**Environment Protection Agency**: an excellent site for young students which explains the mechanics of global warming, etc.
www.epa.gov/globalwarming

**The Environmental Change Research Centre**, University College London:
www.geog.ucl.ac.uk/ecrc

Impacts of climate change on food production:
www.epa.gov/globalwarming/impacts

Information on Bangladesh Floods of 1998:
www.bangladeshonline.com/gob/flood98/ *or* www.bangladeshflood98.org/

Information on extreme weather caused by climate change: www.heatisonline.org/

**Intergovernmental Panel on Climate Change (IPCC):**
www.ipcc.ch

**National Oceanic and Atmospheric Administration**: the impacts of El Niño and La Niña. http://pmel.noaa.gov/toga-tao/el-nino/

**New Scientist**: the Planet Science page provides information and articles on topical issues, including air pollution.
www.newscientist.com

**Reef Check**: a conservation group that monitors the state of the world's coral reefs.
www.reefcheck.org/

**World Health Organization:**
www.who.int/peh/climate/climate_and_health

**World Meteorological Organization**: www.wmo.ch/

**World Resources Institute**: www.wri.org/

## THE CLIMATE CHANGE SCEPTICS:

**Global Climate Coalition**: www.globalclimate.org

**Greening Earth Society**: www.greeningearthsociety.org/

**Fossil Fuels Association**: www.fossilfuels.org/

# INDEX

Numbers in **bold** refer to illustrations.

Africa 7, 21, 24, 34, 42, **42**, 43, **43**, 49
Antarctica 7, 28, **28**, 29
Arctic, the 20, 28, 38
atmosphere 4–8, 10, **10**, 11, **11**, 12, 13, 14, 15, 16, 17, 19, 20–21, 26, 27, 44, 45, 47, 52, 53, 54, 55, **55**, 57
Australia 17, 18, 24, 26, **45**

Bangladesh 26, 31–33, **33**, 41, **48**, 57
Brazil 40, **40**, 48

Canada 18, 28, **38**, **55**
Carbon Club, the 57
carbon dioxide 11, 12, 13, **13**, 36–37, 44, 45, 53, **53**, 54, **54**, 55, 56, 57, 58
emissions 12, **12**, **15**, 52, 53, 55, 56, 57, 58
Caribbean, the 6, 35
Central America 22, 26
CFCs 15
China 12, **12**, 26, 57, **57**
cities **12**, 26, 30, **30-31**, **56**
climate zones 6, **6**, 34
climatologists 20
coasts 5, 17, **17**, 23, 30, **30**
computers 7, 8, 26–27, 52
coral reefs 21, 36, **36**, 37, **37**, 39
bleaching of 36–37, **37**
Costa Rica 34, **34**, 35, **35**, **54**

crops 14, 40–45, 51
coffee 40, **40**
genetically modified 44
rice 14, **14**, 40, **41**, 45
wheat 24, 42, 45, **45**
cyclones 23, **23**, 25

Delta Plan, the 33
developed countries 15, **15**, 25, 49, 52, 57
developing countries 12, 24, 25, 49, 51, 52, 57, 58
droughts 7, **20**, 21, 23, 24, 26, **27**, 33, 42, **42**, 43, 44 45, 47

Earth, the 4–8, **4**, **5**, 10, **10**, 11, 13, 19, 21, 29, 34, 39, 42, 47, 51, 53, 59
El Niño 16–19, **16**, 20, 24, 25, 37, 41
effects of **16**, 19, **19**, 20, 24, **24**, 25, 26, 37, 47
El Niño Southern Oscillation (ENSO) 18–19, 24
energy see also fossil fuels
alternative 53
coal 12, 53, 58
efficiency 53, 54, 55
gas 53
solar 4, **4**, 10, 53
wind 53, **53**
England 51, **52**
Europe 6, 34, 50, 51, 58

farming 13, 14, 31–32, 40, **40**, **41**, 42–45, **45**, 51
fires 13, **15**, **21**, 47

fish/fishing 17, **17**, 30, **37**, 41
floods 4, 8, 22, **22**, 23, **23**, 24, **24**, 25, 26, 31–33, **33**, 41, 47, **48**, **52**, **58**
food shortages 42, **42**, 57
forests 12, 13, **13**, **21**, 24, **34**, **35**, **47**
cloud forests 34, **34**, 35, **35**
destruction of 13, **13**, 21, 47, **47**, 55
rainforests **13**, 24, 34, 39
fossil fuels 12, 13, 14, 53, 56, 57
frosts 40, **40**, **45**

gases 10, **10**, 11, 12, **12**, **14**, 15, 16, 20, 52
see also carbon dioxide
see also greenhouse gases
methane 12, 14, **14**, 55
nitrogen oxide 12, 14
Global Climate Coalition 57
global warming 10, **10**, 11, 13, 15, 20, 22–24, 25, **28**, 35, 37, 42, 43, 52, **52**, 53
greenhouse effect **10**, 12, 14, 30
greenhouse gases **10**, 11, 12, 14, 15, 20, 21, **33**, 52–53, 54, 55, **55**, 57, **57**, 58, 59
Gulf Stream 6

Hague Conference **58**, 59
health, risks to 44, 46–51, **50**
dengue fever 48–49
malaria 49–51
heatwaves 8, 21, 23, 26, 46, **46**

Holland 32, **32**, 44, **58**, 59
homes, destruction of **22**, **23**, **24**, 25, **25**
Honduras **22**
hurricanes 4, 7, **7**, 8, 22, **22**, 23, 25, 47
   Hurricane Linda **7**
   Hurricane Mitch 22, **22**, 26

ice, melting of 20, 28–29, **29**, 39
   ice caps 6, 7, 20, 28
   ice sheets 7
   ice shelves 28, **28**, 29, 38
India **14**, 23, **23**, 24, **25**, 26, 49
   Orissa 23, **23**, **25**
Indonesia 17, 24, 47, **47**
industry 12, **12**, 14, 15, 52, 56, 57
Intergovernmental Panel on Climate Change (IPCC) 9, 10, 11, 20, 26, 28, 30, **33**
irrigation 40, 43, **50**, 51

Japan 58

Kyoto Protocol 58, 59

landslides 22
La Niña 18–20
   effects of **18**, 19, 24

malaria 49–51
meteorologists 6, 8
Mexico **7**, 26, **27**
mosquitoes 48, **49**, 50, 51
mudslides 24, **24**

Netherlands, the 32
New York 30, **30-31**, **56**
North America 18, **18**, 21, 42, 50, 51, 55
North Pole 20
Norway 54, 55

oceans 6, 7, 11, 16–18, 22, 24, 27, 28, 29, 36–37, 41
   Atlantic Ocean 6, 7, 19, 25, 43
   Indian Ocean 19, 24, 37
   Pacific Ocean 16–19, **16**, 20, 24, 37, 41
ocean currents 4, 6, **28**

people, actions of 9, 12, 13, 14, 23, 52–53
Peru 17, **17**, **24**, 41
pollution, air **12**, 15, **15**, 46, 47, **47**, 56, 58–59, **59**
power stations 11, 12, **12**, 53, **59**

rainfall 6, 17–19, 21, 22, **22**, 23, 24, **24**, 25, 31, 40, 41, 42, 43, 45, 47, 49
rainforests see forests
research ships 19, 27
rice see crops
rivers 11, **22**, 31–32, **32**, 35
Russia 12, 20

satellites 6, 7, **7**, 8, 13, 16, 18, 27, 28
sea levels, rise in 28–33, **30**, 57
seasons 5, **5**, 34, **41**, 46
Siberia **29**, 45
soil erosion 24, 42
South America **16**, 17, 41, 48
South-east Asia 40, **41**, 45, **47**
South Pacific islands 30, 32, 57
snow 7, **9**, 25
storms **7**, 22, 25, 32, **32**, 37, 39
Sun, the 4, **4**, 5, **5**, 8, 10, **10**, 11, 15, 27, 42
   energy from 4, **4**, 10, **10**, 53

temperature, changes in 6, 8, 10, 11, 17–18, 20–21, 26–27, 28, **28**, 29, 35, 36, **36**, 37–39, **38**, 40, 42, **45**, 46, **46**, 49, 50
trade winds 16–19, 24
transport 14, **55**, 56, **56**, 57, **57**
   cars 14, 54, **55**, 56, **56**, 57
   public **55**, **57**
   Skytrain **55**
trees 7, 13, 21, 43, 55
   see also forests
tree planting **54**, 55
Tropics, the 4, 6, **13**, 16, 23, 34, 37, 38, 39, 48

UK 12, 18, **50**, 52
USA 6, **9**, 12, 14, 18, 24, 25, **30**, 44, **44**, 46, 47, **53**, 54, 56, **56**, 57, 58, **58**

volcanoes, eruption of 8, 11, **11**

water 21, 33, 35, 36–37, 40, 41, 43, **43**, 44, **44**, 45, 47, **48**
water shortages 21
weather 4, 17–18, **18**, 20, 25–26, 32, 34, 57
   forecasts 4, 6, 26
   stations 6, 7, 18, 26
wildlife 34–39
   birds 34
   butterflies 34
   fish 36, 39, 41
   golden toads 35, **35**, 39
   polar bears **38**, 38–39
wind 4, 6, 16–19, 22, 24, 25, 27
wind farms 53, **53**